DEADLY
2014
ANNUAL

BBC EARTH

DEADLY 2014 ANNUAL

Orion Children's Books

First published in Great Britain in 2013
by Orion Children's Books
a division of the Orion Publishing Group Ltd
Orion House
5 Upper St Martin's Lane
London WC2H 9EA
An Hachette UK Company

1 3 5 7 9 10 8 6 4 2

Derived from and based on the BBC TV series Deadly 60.

Photo credits (b: bottom; t: top; l: left; r: right; c: centre)
11 Deadly 60: Series 3 © Ruth Harries 2012; [12-15 © BBC 2012 tbc]; 17tl & tr © BBC 2009; 18b © BBC 2012; 22 © BBC 2012; 23t & b © BBC 2012; 24 (all pics) © BBC 2010; 25b © BBC 2012; 26t © BBC 2010; 26c Deadly 60: Series 3 © Graham MacFarlane 2012; 26b © BBC 2010; 31t © BBC 2009; 34t Deadly 60: Series 3 © Kirstine Davidson 2012; 35t © BBC 2010; 35c Deadly 60: Series 2 © Graham MacFarlane 2010; 35b Deadly 60: Series 2 © Nikki Waldron 2010; 36t © BBC 2009; 38c © BBC 2009; [40-41 tbc]; 42r © BBC 2009; 43tl Deadly 60: Series 1 © James Brickell 2009; 44 Deadly 60: Series 3 © Elizabeth Sutton 2012; 46 Deadly 60: Series 3 © Elizabeth Sutton 2012; [50-51 tbc]; 52bl Deadly 60: Series 1 © Jason Isley/Scuba Zoo 2009; 52tr © 2009; 52br © BBC 2009; 53t Deadly 60: Series 1 © Adam White 2009; 53c © BBC 2010; 54, 56 & 57 Deadly 60: Series 3 © Katy Elson 2012; 58tr © BBC 2009; 59t © BBC 2009; 61bl © BBC 2010; 62l Deadly 60: Series 3 © Craig Adams 2012; 62tr & br © BBC 2012; 63tr © BBC 2012; 64 Deadly 60: Series 1 © Steve Clark 2009; 67b © BBC 2012; 69 Deadly 60: Series 3 © Kirstine Davidson 2012; 72 Deadly 60: Series 2 © Emma Jones 2010; 74 Deadly 60: Series 3 © Scott Alexander 2012.
Ardea: 6 Duncan Usher; 21 Suzi Eszterhas; 30r Stefan Myers; 31c Jim Zipp; 33c Thomas Dressler; 34b Stefan Myers; 42b M. Watson; 47 Brian Bevan; 59c Auscape; 60tr Wardene Weisser; 61br Jim Zipp; 64bl Hans and Judy Beste; 66 M. Watson. **Daisy O'Neill:** 33t; 36bl & br. **Ingram Publishing:** 30l; 31b; 43tr; 43b; 53b; 60bl; 63 tl; 63br; 68. ***Istockphoto.com***: 42t Alexandr Pakhnyushchyy. **Shutterstock:** 18t Peter Waters; 20 Galyna Andrushko; 32b Jean Patrick Ross; 58bl Andrea Izzotti; 61t Ewan Chesser. **SuperStock:** 17b Nature Picture Library; 25t Minden Pictures; 32t Minden Pictures; 32c Minden Pictures; 39 Flirt; 59b NaturePL; 67t Gohier/VW Pics.

Compiled by Jinny Johnson
Designed by Sue Michniewicz

A catalogue record for this book is available from the British Library.

ISBN 978 1 4440 0656 8

Printed and bound in Germany by Mohn Media

www.orionbooks.co.uk

CONTENTS

Welcome to the 2014 Deadly Annual 11
Our Deadly technology 12
North America: animal facts 16
North American animal wordsearch 19
Portrait of a predator: brown bear 20
Exploring a coral reef 22
Central & South America: animal facts 24
Central & South American animal wordsearch 27
Deadly doodle: Goliath bird-eating spider 28
Deadly special: top 10 lethal weapons 30
Africa: animal facts 34
African animal criss-cross 37
Portrait of a predator: lion 38
Deadly battle: predator v prey Cheetah v Thompson's gazelle 40
Europe: animal facts 42
European animal wordsearch 45
Portrait of a predator: kestrel 46
Deadly doodle: lynx 48
Deadly battle: predator v prey Golden eagle v hare 50
Asia: animal facts 52
Asian animal wordsearch 55
Portrait of a predator: komodo dragon 56
Deadly special: top 10 killer tactics 58
Australasia: animal facts 62
Australasian word scramble 65
Deadly special: animals in danger 66
Quiz crossword 70
Puzzle answers 72

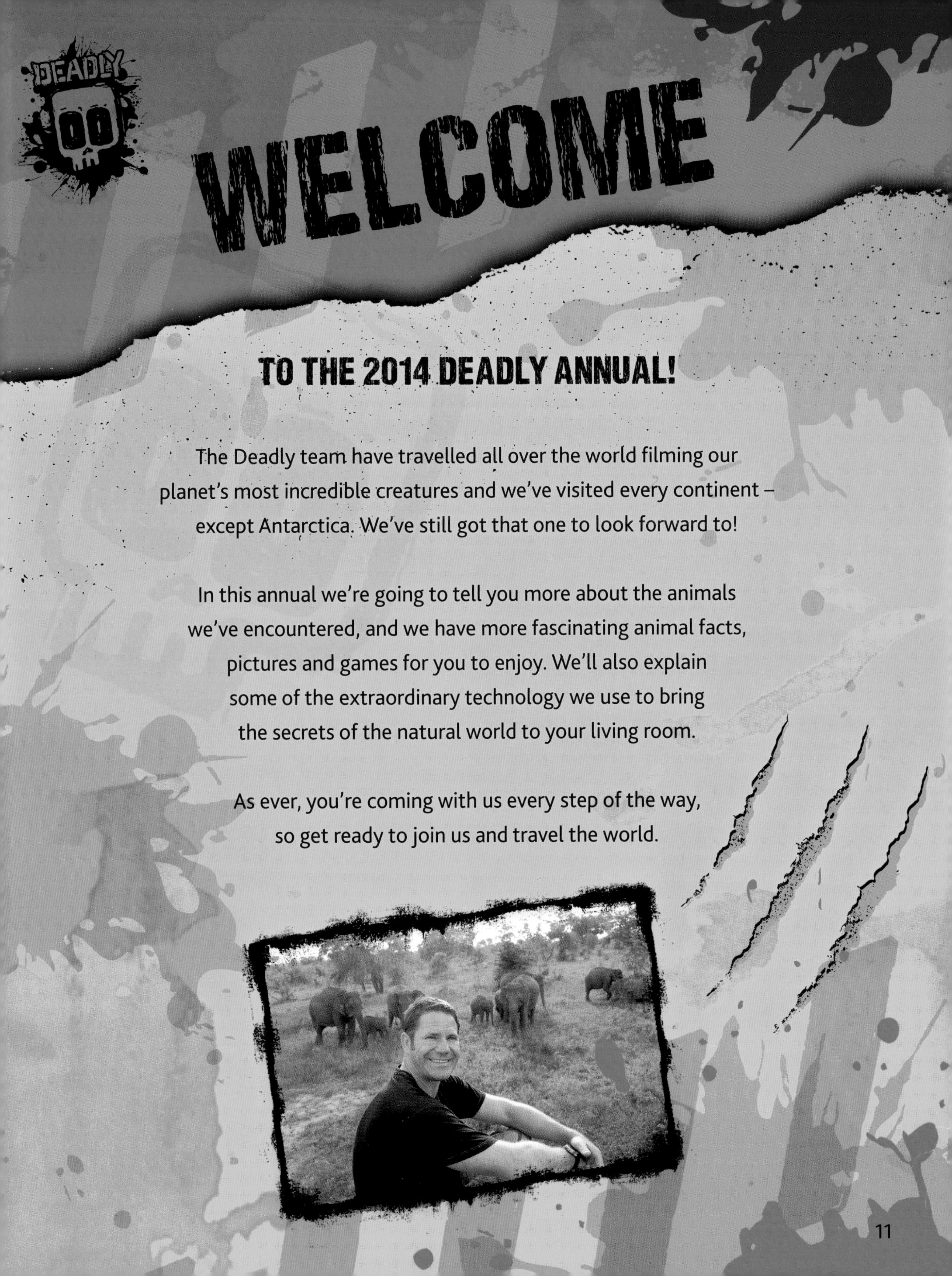

WELCOME

TO THE 2014 DEADLY ANNUAL!

The Deadly team have travelled all over the world filming our planet's most incredible creatures and we've visited every continent – except Antarctica. We've still got that one to look forward to!

In this annual we're going to tell you more about the animals we've encountered, and we have more fascinating animal facts, pictures and games for you to enjoy. We'll also explain some of the extraordinary technology we use to bring the secrets of the natural world to your living room.

As ever, you're coming with us every step of the way, so get ready to join us and travel the world.

OUR DEADLY TECHNOLOGY

In Deadly 60 we film animals in the wild so we can show you their behaviour as it really happens.

But sometimes we need a little extra help to see animal behaviour in ways that the human eye can't manage. That's when we use our Deadly technology to enable us to get the killer shots, bringing you new and exciting views of the natural world.

TIME-LAPSE

When filming behaviour that happens over a long period we sometimes need to speed up the action. A time-lapse camera can be set to run for hours, even days, then the results are speeded up. With one of these cameras we can show you changes that would take too long to watch in real time.

When hours are condensed to minutes we can watch and understand behaviour such as spiders spinning webs, starfish hunting and carnivorous plants trapping prey.

HIGH-SPEED CAMERA

Some of the most exciting aspects of animal behaviour are over in the blink of an eye – actions like a chameleon's super-fast tongue shooting out to catch an insect or a great white shark lunging from the water to attack a seal.

For these moments, the high-speed camera, which can shoot thousands of frames a second, is invaluable. Once the footage is slowed down, you can see such lightning-fast actions as a snake's strike – or Steve bursting a balloon of water! In reality it's over in a fraction of a second, but we see it in slow-motion detail.

INFRARED CAMERA

Many animals choose to be active at night and come out when it is completely dark, making it hard for us to film what's happening. We can use spotlights but these sometimes disturb and frighten away creatures. Much more effective are infrared cameras which have sensors that pick up a different wavelength to visible light. With the help of infrared lights, these cameras can capture images in total darkness.

With these kinds of cameras we can film predators hunting at night – something we would never be able to see normally. We can also film inside the darkest caves, exploring the lives of creatures such as bats.

CAMERA TRAP

This has proved a vital part of our equipment over the years. It's a camera with a motion sensor that we can leave watching for the action while we go off to bed! Any animal that passes through the motion sensor is going to get filmed. We used camera traps in Peru when we were trying to film caimans on land. We left several camera traps in place overnight with some bait nearby. In the morning we returned to find incredible footage of a huge black caiman enjoying the midnight feast we'd left for him.

THERMAL-IMAGING CAMERA

This is a very special piece of kit, which captures not light, but temperature. On this camera, cool things appear as blue, warm as orange, and hot as white. This camera is great for tracking animals at night and also helps us to understand how some predators might find their prey in darkness. For example, some snakes, such as pit vipers, have their own 'thermal imaging'. A pit viper has heat-sensitive pits on its head and so can 'see' the heat given off by warm-blooded prey like mice and rats. This makes it easy for the snake to track and catch its meal at night, even in complete darkness.

MINI-CAM

These tiny cameras allow us to get up close to creatures and film them in fantastic detail. We've placed one on a wildebeest skull to watch vultures at work. We've even trained a goshawk to fly wearing a harness carrying a tiny onboard camera, giving us a real bird's eye view as she went about her deadly business of hunting.

We can also fix a mini-cam on to a truck, boat or microlight so you can come with us wherever we go.

NORTH AMERICA: ANIMAL FACTS

BISON are the largest land animals in North America. Once they roamed freely over much of the continent, but now they are usually only seen in nature reserves. Bison feed on grass and other plants, but their huge size makes them formidable animals. They grow up to 3.5 metres long and can weigh as much as 1,000 kilograms. Despite their bulk, bison are surprisingly speedy and can run at up to 60 kilometres an hour.

The **WOLVERINE** belongs to the weasel family and is one of the fiercest hunters in North America. It attacks caribou and other animals many times its own size. A wolverine's jaws are so strong that it can bite through the frozen flesh of animals it finds buried in the snow.

The **CALIFORNIA SEA LION** is the speediest of all sea lions and can swim at an amazing 40 kilometres an hour as it chases prey. It dives deep and can stay underwater for nearly 10 minutes without coming up for air.

SEA OTTERS live in the North Pacific where the water is very cold. Fortunately, the sea otter has one of the thickest coats of any animal, with 100,000 hairs or more per square centimetre.

The fastest running animal in North America is the **PRONGHORN**, an animal that looks similar to an antelope. It can run at 86 kilometres an hour when escaping from predators – that's much faster than the speediest humans in the world.

The **BALD EAGLE** is a huge bird of prey found throughout North America. The eagle's wings measure up to 2.4 metres from tip to tip and it weighs as much as 6.3 kilograms. It hunts fish as well as other birds, mammals and reptiles and will also take carrion – animals that are already dead.

The bald eagle makes one of the biggest nests of any bird. The nests are used year after year and the biggest recorded measured more than 6 metres deep – taller than a giraffe!

The **POLAR BEAR** is one of the largest land carnivores in the world. It lives in the Arctic and can survive temperatures of about -45°C, which is much colder than your freezer.

One of the deadliest snakes in North America is the **EASTERN DIAMONDBACK RATTLESNAKE**. The world's largest rattlesnake, it can grow up to 2.4 metres long and can reach out about two-thirds of its body length when striking at prey or defending itself.

SKUNKS are probably the smelliest animals in North America. If attacked, a skunk will squirt out liquid from glands under its tail. This liquid can travel 2 or 3 metres, smells terrible and also causes burning pain in the victim's eyes and nose. Once a predator experiences that, they don't tend to approach a skunk again!

AMERICAN ALLIGATORS are noisy animals and make lots of bellowing and roaring calls. The young even call out from inside their eggs when they are ready to hatch!

The **BLACK WIDOW SPIDER** is one of the most venomous spiders in North America. The female is about twice the size of the male and has red or orange markings on her body.

Black widows make webs to trap caterpillars, flies, beetles and other insects.

The **GREY WOLF** is the largest member of the dog family. A full-grown male is up to 1.65 metres long and weighs as much as 50 kilograms. Females are slightly smaller. Expert predators, wolves hunt in packs and bring down animals that are 10 times their own size, such as bison.

DEADLY 60

NORTH AMERICAN ANIMAL WORDSEARCH

These are just some of the incredible creatures that live in North America. Can you find their names in this wordsearch?

N	E	M	C	Y	K	N	D	E	I	A	Q	R	A	P
O	N	R	T	O	A	N	T	T	L	R	F	A	E	S
I	I	F	E	E	T	S	U	L	E	L	S	E	L	R
L	R	M	E	T	L	T	I	K	O	A	T	B	G	E
N	E	U	H	I	T	G	O	W	S	T	F	K	A	T
I	V	B	A	C	A	O	Y	N	D	E	Y	C	E	S
A	L	F	M	T	O	E	A	O	M	D	O	A	D	N
T	O	R	O	H	R	E	T	E	E	O	P	L	L	O
N	W	R	H	G	I	C	A	T	S	R	U	B	A	M
U	E	K	A	N	S	E	L	T	T	A	R	T	B	A
O	P	O	L	A	R	B	E	A	R	C	N	E	H	L
M	X	O	F	C	I	T	C	R	A	C	I	E	U	I
T	L	H	H	X	N	I	C	R	L	O	F	Y	O	G
E	O	F	R	A	S	T	N	A	W	O	A	E	A	O
M	N	A	E	E	N	A	I	T	U	N	S	T	N	S

WOLVERINE
BALD EAGLE
SKUNK

MOUNTAIN LION
COTTONMOUTH
RATTLESNAKE

RACCOON
ARCTIC FOX
SEA OTTER

BLACK BEAR
ALLIGATOR
GREY WOLF

POLAR BEAR
GILA MONSTER

PORTRAIT OF A PREDATOR: BROWN BEAR

Brown bears are among the largest predatory animals in North America.

These huge creatures feed on anything from grass, nuts and berries to fish, birds and other animals. They even sometimes attack large hoofed mammals, such as moose and elk.

Brown bears generally live alone, except for mothers and cubs, but they gather at rivers to catch salmon as they swim upstream to spawn.

A bear may eat as much as 40 kilograms of salmon a day during this period which fattens it up nicely before it hibernates through the winter months. A bear may hibernate for as long as 6 months without eating anything at all.

Brown bears live in northern North America and in parts of northern Europe and Asia.

Grizzly bears are a subspecies of brown bear found in Alaska and parts of Canada. They are named for their silver-tipped fur.

Largest of all the brown bears are Kodiak bears, another subspecies, which live on the Kodiak Islands off the coast of Alaska. These giants can weigh up to 780 kilograms – more than 10 people – but most brown bears are smaller and lighter than this.

Large head.
Strong body with big, powerful shoulders.
Thick fur.
Long claws for digging.

EXPLORING A CORAL REEF

When the Deadly team filmed in Mexico we took the chance to explore the coral reef off the east coast. This is the second longest in the world after Australia's Great Barrier Reef.

It's a magnificent wonderland with many types of coral, incredibly brightly coloured fish and many other creatures. There is so much life there and so much diversity. But as usual we were looking for contenders to go on our Deadly 60 list.

First off was a **NURSE SHARK** – a species that is rather different from other sharks.

It's not a streamlined speedster constantly on the move but spends much of its time lying on the seabed. At night it goes hunting on the reef and uses the 2 sets of sensitive barbels on its nose to help it search out prey such as crabs, sea urchins and shrimp.

Another predatory reef dweller is the **BLACK GROUPER** – one of the bigger fish on the reef. It has a large mouth and huge lips which it uses to swallow smaller fish. It grows up to 1.5 metres long.

But the fish we were most excited to see was a **GREEN MORAY EEL** – a creature that is more than 2 metres long and has a mouthful of impressive teeth.

A stealthy predator, it conceals itself in a crevice on the reef and lies in wait to ambush unwary creatures as they pass.

This fish has 4 nostrils, 2 of them on little tubes on its nose, giving it an incredibly good sense of smell. This helps it pick up the tiniest scents from the water and alerts it to prey close by.

A menacing monster with a huge muscular body, the green moray is truly a candidate for our Deadly 60.

CENTRAL & SOUTH AMERICA: ANIMAL FACTS

At about 120 kilograms in weight, the **JAGUAR** is the largest cat in the Americas. Its jaws are so strong that it can even bite through turtle shells. Relative to its size, the jaguar probably has the strongest bite of all big cats.

The **HARPY EAGLE** is the largest eagle in South America and one of the most powerful of all birds of prey. Its wings measure as much as 2.2 metres when fully spread and it has a big hooked beak and talons as long as a bear's claws. It hunts high in the rainforest canopy, catching monkeys, sloths and other animals.

The **VAMPIRE BAT** is the only mammal that feeds entirely on blood. It makes a wound on its victim's skin with its sharp teeth and laps up about a teaspoonful of blood at each feed.

The biggest of all anteaters, the **GIANT ANTEATER** is up to 2 metres long, but it feeds only on small creatures such as ants and termites. However, it can eat more than 30,000 of these little insects every day. It catches its prey with its long sticky tongue, which measures up to 50 centimetres long.

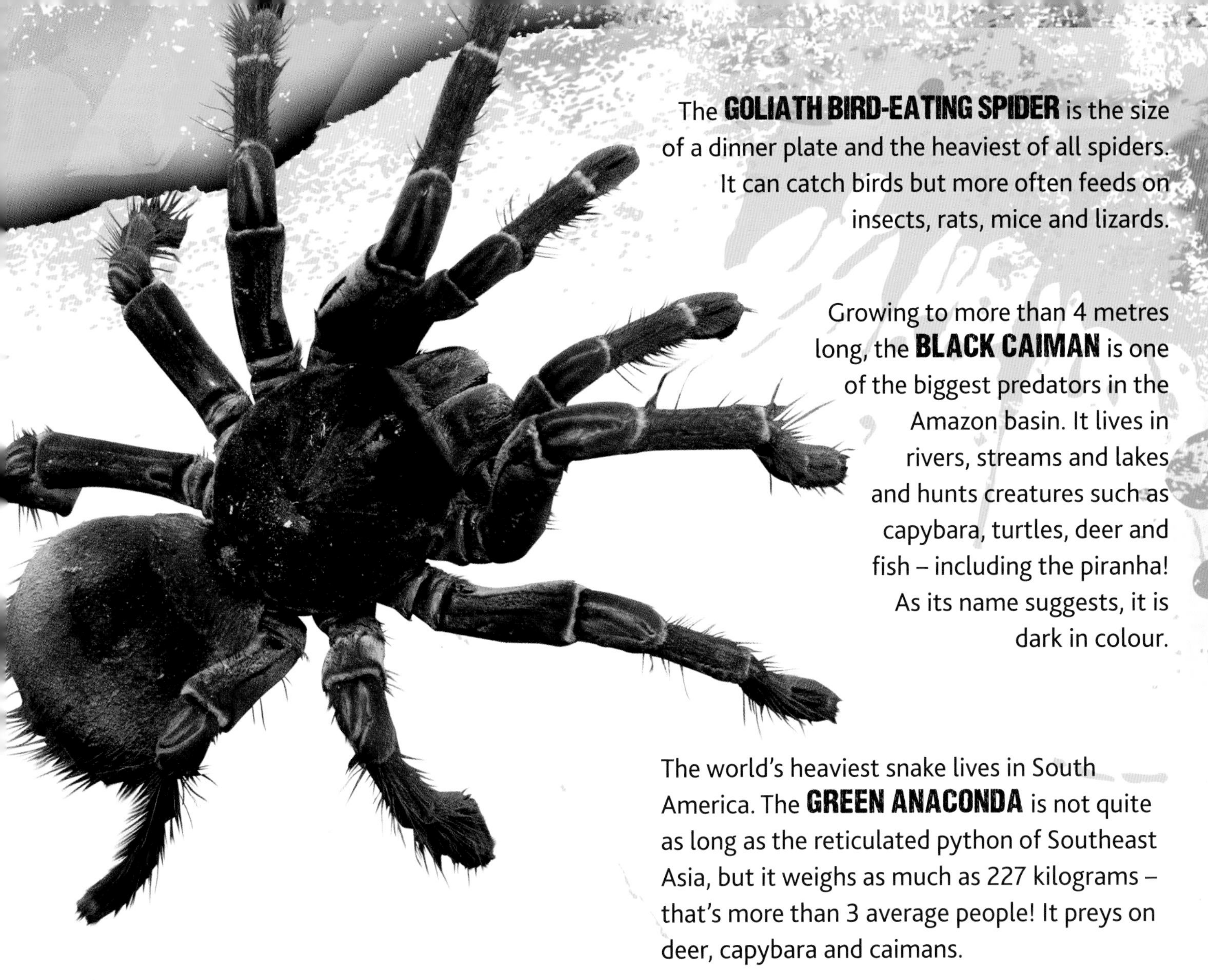

The **GOLIATH BIRD-EATING SPIDER** is the size of a dinner plate and the heaviest of all spiders. It can catch birds but more often feeds on insects, rats, mice and lizards.

Growing to more than 4 metres long, the **BLACK CAIMAN** is one of the biggest predators in the Amazon basin. It lives in rivers, streams and lakes and hunts creatures such as capybara, turtles, deer and fish – including the piranha! As its name suggests, it is dark in colour.

The world's heaviest snake lives in South America. The **GREEN ANACONDA** is not quite as long as the reticulated python of Southeast Asia, but it weighs as much as 227 kilograms – that's more than 3 average people! It preys on deer, capybara and caimans.

The **SPECTACLED BEAR** is the only bear in South America and the second largest land mammal on the continent. It eats lots of plants and catches rodents, birds and insects. This bear gets its name from the white markings around its eyes.

The **ELECTRIC EEL** really does make its own electricity. It gives off bursts of electricity of up to 600 volts to attack prey and to defend itself from attackers. It may also use its electric powers to find its way in the murky waters where it lives – like a kind of natural radar.

Lots of kinds of **POISON DART FROGS** live in the rainforests of Central and South America. All have poisonous secretions in their skin but the most deadly of all is the golden poison dart frog, which may be the most poisonous of all vertebrate animals. This frog is only 5 centimetres long but its skin could contain enough poison to kill 22,000 mice.

ARMY ANTS are tiny insects but they move in huge swarms that may number more than 200,000 individuals. They march over the forest floor, attacking any prey that crosses their path. They hunt as a group and can overcome animals much larger than themselves.

The **BOA CONSTRICTOR** is not a venomous snake. It kills its prey by wrapping its strong body around its victim and squeezing so hard that the prey cannot breathe and eventually suffocates. The boa constrictor then swallows its meal whole – but it may take as long as 4 or even 6 days to digest big prey. These snakes can swallow animals as large as wild pigs.

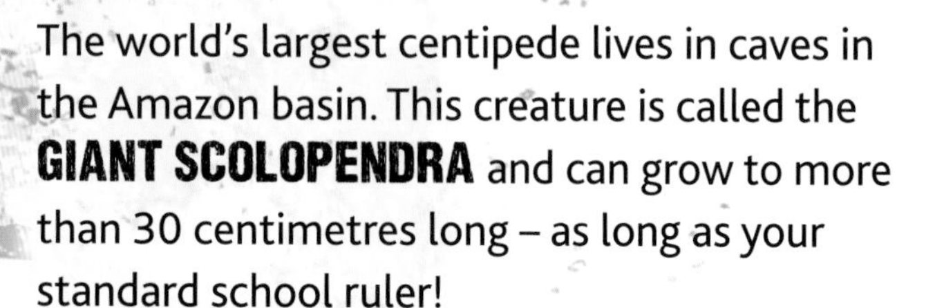

The world's largest centipede lives in caves in the Amazon basin. This creature is called the **GIANT SCOLOPENDRA** and can grow to more than 30 centimetres long – as long as your standard school ruler!

CENTRAL & SOUTH AMERICAN ANIMAL WORDSEARCH

These are just some of the incredible creatures that live in Central and South America. Can you find their names in this wordsearch?

R	B	S	B	A	N	A	Q	T	O	C	E	L	O	T
I	E	U	L	V	E	D	Z	N	D	H	O	M	P	L
F	E	T	S	K	O	N	W	A	B	S	A	O	E	C
H	L	N	A	H	E	O	S	Y	Y	K	L	E	F	S
A	R	O	K	E	M	C	K	M	F	I	C	G	V	N
R	S	H	W	K	T	A	U	R	B	I	B	T	C	P
P	I	O	T	D	P	N	S	A	R	M	U	J	Y	R
Y	F	K	J	V	E	A	A	T	K	W	G	O	A	F
E	S	H	Z	N	I	N	C	T	E	C	U	U	O	B
A	M	F	V	O	H	E	A	E	N	R	G	E	H	W
G	D	G	M	N	L	E	X	M	B	A	A	F	C	Y
L	Z	P	H	E	S	R	C	I	J	Z	I	Y	O	Q
E	H	T	F	W	M	G	P	R	U	A	K	G	E	P
S	B	G	R	B	L	A	C	K	C	A	I	M	A	N
T	A	B	E	R	I	P	M	A	V	F	Y	S	B	R

ARMY ANT
HARPY EAGLE
MANED WOLF
GIANT ANTEATER
ELECTRIC EEL
BUSHMASTER
JAGUAR
OCELOT
BLACK CAIMAN
VAMPIRE BAT
GREEN ANACONDA

Goliath Bird-Eating Spider

Skill Level: Medium

This South American spider is a tarantula and one of the biggest of all spiders. Despite its name, this spider doesn't often eat birds and usually hunts insects and other small creatures. If attacked, the spider bites with fangs that can be up to 2.5 centimetres long. It also flicks tiny barbed hairs at its enemy.

1. First draw a large egg shape on your page. Then add two long egg shapes inside the big one. Add a circle on top of them and draw two small circles inside for the eyes.

2. Add two little upside-down L shapes below the eyes for the palps. Then draw in four big legs on each side of the body.

3. Take a felt-tip pen and draw in the deadly fangs at the front of the head. Go round the eyes in pen. Then go over the legs with thick jaggedy lines to make them look lovely and furry.

4. Continue going over the legs on the other side of your bird-eating spider, making them look as furry as you can.

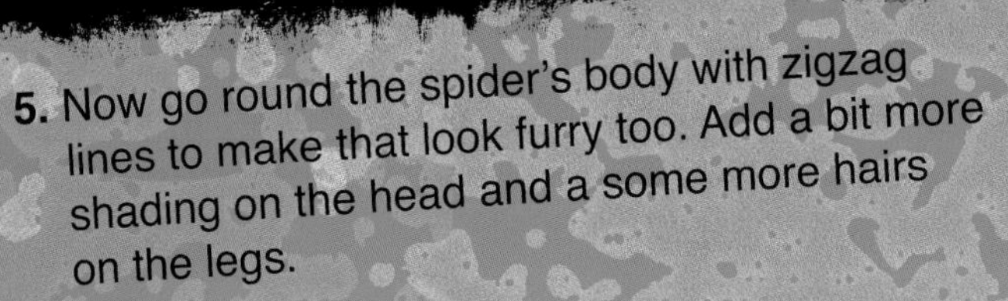

5. Now go round the spider's body with zigzag lines to make that look furry too. Add a bit more shading on the head and a some more hairs on the legs.

6. Finally, rub out your pencil guidelines and there's your deadly bird-eating spider.

DEADLY SPECIAL: TOP 10 LETHAL WEAPONS

Here is the Deadly team's list of the animals that we think have the top 10 lethal weapons in the natural world. We looked at super-sharp talons, extra-strong stings – and some other surprising tricks along the way.

PRAYING MANTIS

Lethal weapon:
killer spines and mouthparts

The mantis may be less than 15 centimetres long but it's armed with monstrous weapons. With sharp spines on its limbs for trapping prey and powerful mouthparts, a mantis can demolish animals twice its size. Mantids are also masters of disguise and some resemble flowers, leaves, even pebbles to help themselves stay invisible to prey – and predators.

GRIZZLY BEAR

Lethal weapon:
claws

Built like a tank and equipped with massive teeth and claws, the grizzly bear is a top predator – although it also eats nuts and berries. It uses its strong claws to hook fish such as salmon from rivers and to dig clams out of the sand on the seashore.

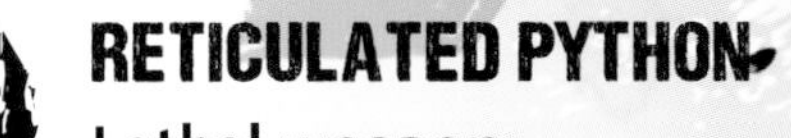

3 RETICULATED PYTHON

Lethal weapon: muscle power

This reptile has a killer squeeze like the boa constrictor but is even longer! In fact it is the longest snake in the world with a record length of 9 metres. The python wraps its powerful coils around its prey and, as the prey breathes out, squeezes tighter and tighter until the victim suffocates. The python also has hyper-flexible jaws that allow it to swallow prey much larger than itself and it can digest the whole animal – even its hooves and horns.

4 GREAT GREY OWL

Lethal weapon: hearing

Exceptional hearing is this bird's deadly weapon, allowing it to pick up the slightest sound of rodents moving on the ground – even when they're under the snow. The structure of the owl's face and feathers acts like a satellite dish to collect and amplify any tiny noise. It then swoops silently to seize its prey in sharp talons and rarely misses its target.

5 VENUS FLYTRAP

Lethal weapon: trigger mechanism

It's not only animals that are ferocious – some plants can be too. The Venus flytrap is the piranha of the plant kingdom and catches insects in its leafy jaws. The plant oozes nectar to attract insects. If an insect brushes against more than one of the tiny hairs on the inner surface of a leaf it triggers a mechanism that snaps the leaf shut and imprisons the victim. The insect is then digested by the plant.

BULLET ANT

Lethal weapon: sting

This little creature has what is probably the most painful sting of any insect. It gets its name from the fact that being stung by one is said to be like being hit by a bullet. Although bullet ants are only up to 2.5 centimetres long they are among the largest of all ants. They use their stings to attack prey and defend themselves against predators.

AYE-AYE

Lethal weapon: finger

A small primate, the aye-aye lives in Madagascar and is active at night. Its special weapon is the very long thin third finger on each of its hands which it uses to winkle out insect larvae from wood. First, the aye-aye taps on tree trunks and listens for any movement of insect larvae under the bark. Once it hears something, the aye-aye tears into the bark with its sharp teeth and extracts the prey with its deadly finger.

QUEEN SNAKE

Lethal weapon: tongue

This snake lives in rivers in parts of North America and feeds mostly on crayfish. Crayfish can be tricky to catch as they have hard shells and sharp pincers. But every 3 or 4 weeks they moult and grow a new shell, and the queen snake is an expert at catching them just when they've shed their hard shells. The queen snake's forked tongue is super-sensitive and can detect the different chemicals a crayfish gives off when it has moulted. With the help of its tongue, the snake catches the soft crayfish and swallows them whole.

9 AFRICAN ELEPHANT

Lethal weapon: tusks

Elephants don't just use their mighty tusks for digging for food and stripping bark from trees. In fights between rival males, the tusks become deadly weapons and can cause serious injuries. Tusks are modified teeth and grow throughout an elephant's life. A tusk can grow to 3 metres long and weigh more than an adult human. Male and female African elephants have tusks but those of the males are larger and heavier.

10 AFRICAN FISH EAGLE

Lethal weapon: talons

This deadly hunter's main weapons are its huge talons which it relies on for catching prey. The eagle patrols lakes and rivers, then swoops low and thrusts its sharp-clawed feet forward to seize its prey. It also uses its talons to catch smaller birds in the air. The fish eagle is such a skilled predator that it can spend as little as 10 minutes a day hunting.

DEADLY 60 AFRICA: ANIMAL FACTS

The **SAVANNA ELEPHANT**, one of the 2 types of African elephant, is the largest land mammal in the world. The biggest known male weighed about 10,000 kilograms – as much as 4 trucks – and stood 4 metres tall at the shoulder. Most male African elephants weigh about 6,000 kilograms and females about 3,000 kilograms.

Even a baby elephant is a heavyweight. At birth, an African elephant weighs 90–120 kilograms, which is more than most people.

And did you know that the ears of every elephant are slightly different in shape?

The **CHEETAH** is the fastest of all land animals. It can run at an incredible 100 kilometres an hour or so – but only for a few hundred metres. Even top Olympic athletes can only manage speeds of about 37 kilometres an hour for short bursts.

AFRICAN WILD DOGS are fast runners too. They run at speeds of up to 55 kilometres an hour when hunting prey and can keep going for long distances.

The **SPOTTED HYENA** has such strong jaws and teeth that it can even crunch through bones, eating every scrap of its prey.

GORILLAS are the biggest of all the primates – the group of animals that contains monkeys, apes and us. A full-grown male gorilla stands up to 1.8 metres tall and weighs twice as much as an average human.

The **AARDVARK** has a tongue that can extend up to 30 centimetres. It uses its tongue to gather termites and can gobble as many as 50,000 of these insects every night.

Despite weighing as much as 1,400 kilograms the **BLACK RHINOCEROS** can run at 55 kilometres an hour and will charge enemies if threatened. Its horns are made of keratin, the same material as your hair and fingernails. The name rhinoceros means 'nose horn'.

The **BLACK MAMBA** is one of the most dangerous snakes in Africa. It typically grows up to 3 metres long and can inject large amounts of highly toxic and fast-acting venom when it strikes its prey. The mamba is also one of the fastest snakes and can move at speeds of 20 kilometres an hour for short distances.

The **GOLIATH FROG**, which lives in West Africa, is the largest frog in the world. It weighs more than 3 kilograms – almost as much as a pet cat.

The **GABOON VIPER** is a venomous snake and an impressive predator. Its fangs can grow to 5 centimetres long and it delivers more venom per strike than any other snake.

At up to 6 metres long, the **NILE CROCODILE** is the biggest reptile in Africa – and one of the most deadly. It spends much of its life in the water but can also move surprisingly fast on land. Fish are its main food but it also attacks large animals such as zebra and buffalo when they come to the water's edge to drink.

A Nile crocodile can eat as much as 25 kilograms of meat at one meal. That's like us eating 100 or more steaks.

Did you know that no two **LEOPARDS** have the same pattern of spots? Each animal is different.

The **FAT-TAILED SCORPION** is up to 15 centimetres long and one of the few species that is dangerous to humans.

Standing well over 5 metres high, the **GIRAFFE** is the tallest animal not only in Africa but also the world. Although these animals are peaceful plant eaters most of the time, rival males engage in fierce battles and cause serious wounds to one another.

The **HIPPOPOTAMUS** feeds only on plants but its huge size and unpredictable nature make it a dangerous animal. A full-grown male weighs as much as 3,200 kilograms and is up to 5.4 metres long with a 50 centimetre tail. The hippo spends most of its life in the water where it moves surprisingly gracefully, but it comes on to land at night to graze.

DEADLY 60

AFRICAN ANIMAL CRISS-CROSS

Can you fill in this criss-cross puzzle with the names of these African animals?

TOP TIP: start with the shortest and longest words.

4 letters
LION

5 letters
FOSSA

7 letters
LEOPARD
GORILLA
CHEETAH
MEERKAT
WARTHOG

8 letters
ELEPHANT
AARDVARK

9 letters
CHAMELEON

10 letters
CHIMPANZEE
SIDEWINDER

12 letters
HIPPOPOTAMUS

PORTRAIT OF A PREDATOR: LION

Lions are the biggest cat in Africa and the only members of the cat family that live in social groups. These groups, called prides, contain a number of related females and their young, led by one or more males.

A full-grown male lion can weigh up to 240 kilograms – more than 3 average people. Females are smaller and weigh up to 180 kilograms or so.

Female lions do most of the hunting for the pride, but males patrol the territory and protect the group. The lionesses hunt together, enabling them to target animals such as buffalo which are 3 times the size of a lion. They cooperate to select a victim and bring it down, often killing with a bite to the throat. The rest of the pride share in the kill.

A full-grown lion is up to 2.5 metres long with a tail of up to a metre.
Only male lions have a mane – a fringe of long hair around the head.
Large canine teeth, claws and teamwork are the lion's main weapons for killing prey. Their powerful jaw muscles allow them to inflict a deadly bite.
Sharp claws can be pulled back (retracted) into fleshy sheaths to protect them when not in use.

DEADLY BATTLE: PREDATOR v PREY
CHEETAH v THOMPSON'S GAZELLE

Predators like the cheetah have to hunt and catch food if they are to survive, but prey animals, such as gazelles, have their own strategies for escaping their deadly enemies and taking care of themselves.

We looked at this life and death struggle in the Masai Mara in East Africa. This is a vast area of open grassland where gazelle graze and predators come to find prey.

PREDATOR

The cheetah is a true athlete and the fastest of all land animals. Light for its size, it has lighter bones and a smaller head than other big cats, as well as an extremely flexible spine and joints. It can reach speeds of around 100 kilometres an hour and has superb acceleration.

A cheetah also has excellent vision and can see prey up to 5 kilometres away. Last but not least, it has sharp curving claws that make lethal weapons.

PREY

The gazelle can't quite match the cheetah's speed, although it is a fast runner. It does, however, have superb stamina and can keep going for longer distances than the cat. It's helped in this by its large windpipe and heart, which allow it to take in plenty of oxygen and

pump it round its body with great efficiency. It is also a skilled escape artist, capable of outmanouevering the cheetah. Who do you think will win this deadly battle?

THE ACTION

Thanks to its keen eyesight the cheetah spots a herd of gazelle from a distance and gets as close as it can to select its victim. Once the choice is made, the cheetah starts to run, reaching a speed of about 100 kilometres an hour in less than 3 seconds. When it's running at full stretch the cheetah spends as much as half the time with all 4 feet off the ground.

But the gazelle doesn't make life easy for the cheetah. It is running at top speed too, making sharp twists and turns to try and escape its hunter. The longer the chase lasts, the harder it gets for the cheetah to succeed – if it doesn't make the kill within about 300 metres the cat may start to overheat, which can be fatal. Most chases last less than a minute.

The cheetah is almost at the limit of its endurance but just manages to get close enough to take a swipe at the gazelle with

its paw. The cat's sharp dewclaw tears a deep wound in the gazelle's leg and it falls to the ground.

The battle is over and this time the cheetah moves in for the kill.

Next time it might not be so lucky.

EUROPE: ANIMAL FACTS

Did you know that it takes about 10 million trips by worker **HONEYBEES** to collect enough nectar from flowers to make a 450 gram jar of honey? Each worker may only live for a few weeks.

The **GREAT RAFT SPIDER** is the largest spider in Britain. It is a wonderfully adaptable predator and can skate over the surface of water, dive to catch tadpoles and even stay underwater for as long as an hour.

Spotty red and black **LADYBIRDS** are actually fierce little predators. They hunt aphids, tiny bugs that feed on plants and can cause lots of damage. One ladybird can eat as many as 5,000 aphids during its life so these insects are very popular with gardeners.

DRAGONFLIES are some of the fastest moving of all insects. They can fly at around 40 kilometres an hour as they zoom through the air hunting other insects.

The **GANNET** is a large seabird which makes spectacular plunge-dives into the sea to catch fish. It swoops over the water looking for prey. When it spots something, the gannet folds its wings back to make its body as streamlined as a torpedo as it dives from as high as 30 metres above the surface. It enters the water at speeds of up to 95 kilometres an hour and seizes its prey in its long sharp beak.

The **ADDER** lives in Europe and parts of Asia and is the only venomous snake in Britain. It is also the only snake that lives inside the Arctic Circle. The adder uses its venom to kill voles, mice, young birds and other prey.

The **GARDEN SPIDER** spins webs that may measure up to 40 centimetres across to catch its prey. An average web contains as much as 30 metres of silk. The female's body measures up to 18 millimetres across but the male is only 9 millimetres.

The **PEREGRINE FALCON** is the fastest animal ever known to have lived. It dives through the sky to catch other birds and moves at speeds of as much 200 kilometres an hour. These birds are widespread around the world and live in parts of North and South America, Africa, Asia and Australia as well as Europe.

OTTERS belong to the weasel family and are fast, expert swimmers which spend most of their time in the water. They have webbed feet to help them swim and can close off their ears and nose when underwater. A full-grown otter weighs up to 10 kilograms and is up to 70 centimetres long with a thick tail of up to 40 centimetres.

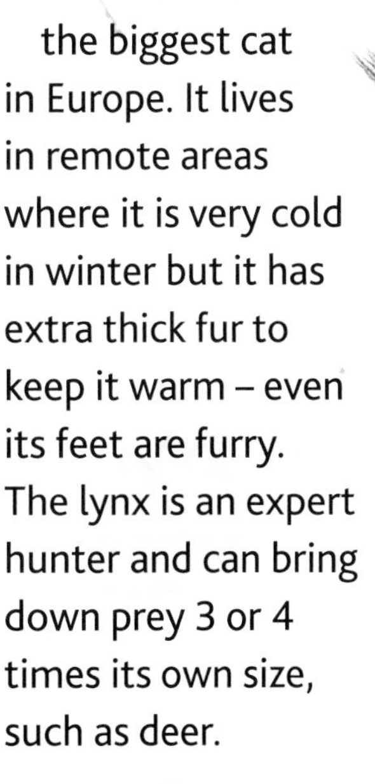

The **LYNX** is the biggest cat in Europe. It lives in remote areas where it is very cold in winter but it has extra thick fur to keep it warm – even its feet are furry. The lynx is an expert hunter and can bring down prey 3 or 4 times its own size, such as deer.

STEVE MEETS SOME FRIENDLY RATS.

EUROPEAN ANIMAL WORDSEARCH

These are just some of the incredible creatures that live in Europe. Can you find their names in this wordsearch?

S	R	L	C	R	T	N	N	D	L	C	T	F	M	N
I	X	A	O	E	H	F	R	S	R	E	D	E	W	I
R	O	H	N	R	L	A	R	A	C	H	A	T	E	A
U	O	N	H	E	G	H	B	O	I	A	E	E	A	R
I	A	R	M	O	A	S	N	K	X	N	Y	L	E	W
G	I	O	N	S	P	G	O	Y	W	S	T	M	T	O
E	L	F	E	I	E	A	H	T	C	A	T	R	H	D
O	L	K	D	R	H	O	R	N	E	T	H	C	I	R
Y	I	E	E	A	I	A	H	D	N	M	N	S	N	R
P	R	E	L	E	R	T	S	E	K	R	T	E	O	S
O	L	U	E	S	E	L	P	A	E	C	E	R	N	G
E	L	G	A	E	Y	N	W	A	T	M	E	D	T	M
E	E	C	I	E	R	H	H	E	A	T	N	P	D	S
T	O	R	S	T	O	I	O	N	T	M	S	C	R	A
M	I	D	W	T	D	T	A	O	O	D	I	H	N	T

KESTREL
GANNET
GOSHAWK
CONGER EEL
HORNET
OTTER
DRAGONFLY
ADDER
LYNX
TAWNY EAGLE
CRAB SPIDER
PIKE

PORTRAIT OF A PREDATOR: KESTREL

Small but powerful, the kestrel is a member of the falcon family. It is one of the most common birds of prey in Britain and throughout Europe.

One of the secrets of the kestrel's success as a hunter is its ability to hover above the ground, choosing just the right moment to plunge down and seize prey. The bird achieves this by flying into the wind so the air is constantly driven under its wings, creating lift. It moves its wings only slightly to keep aloft while its head remains still, watching for prey.

The kestrel has superb eyesight that is probably 8 times more powerful than ours. It also has another very special skill in that it can see ultra-violet light and this is important. Voles are one of the kestrel's main prey and these little creatures leave a trail of urine behind them as they scurry around in the grass. The urine glows in ultra-violet light, allowing the kestrel to follow its prey as it moves around on the ground and pinpoint its strike with ease.

Ultra-violet vision.
Ability to hover above the ground and hang almost effortlessly in mid-air.
Excellent eyesight for spotting prey from the air.
Sharp talons for seizing prey.

Lynx Skill Level: Easy

This prowling, pouncing predator is the largest cat in Europe. Its excellent hearing and sharp teeth help it to catch animals that are three or four times its size, such as deer.

1. Draw a big hill in the middle of your paper. Add two triangles for the ears and a cup shape for the mouth. Draw a triangle for the nose and two more for the eyes.

2. Using a black marker, add in some detail. Draw round the ears, giving them more shape and add a line to make the flap. Add some tufts at the tips of the ears.

3. For the fur around the lynx's head, draw some simple zigzag shapes at the top of the head and add some larger zigzags at the sides. Go over the pencil lines for the mouth with your marker pen.

4. Draw a big box inside the mouth shape and add in those big sharp teeth, two at the top and two smaller ones at the bottom. Add a little shading inside the mouth. Go over the nose and eyes in marker pen and add lines linking the nose to the eyes. Draw in some extra-thick lines over the eyes.

5. Add little lines inside the eyes for the pupils and draw in some markings around the eyes – a bit like eyelashes. Then add a line either side of the nose to emphasise the top of the mouth.

6. To finish off your doodle, draw some little dots and long lines on either side of the nose for the whiskers.Then add in a little shading on the nose of your ferocious-looking lynx.

DEADLY BATTLE: PREDATOR v PREY
GOLDEN EAGLE v HARE

There's a constant race between predators and prey, as the hunters struggle to find enough food and the victims do their best to avoid their killer tactics. This life and death battle took place in the wild highlands of Scotland, where golden eagles fly and hares race around on the ground.

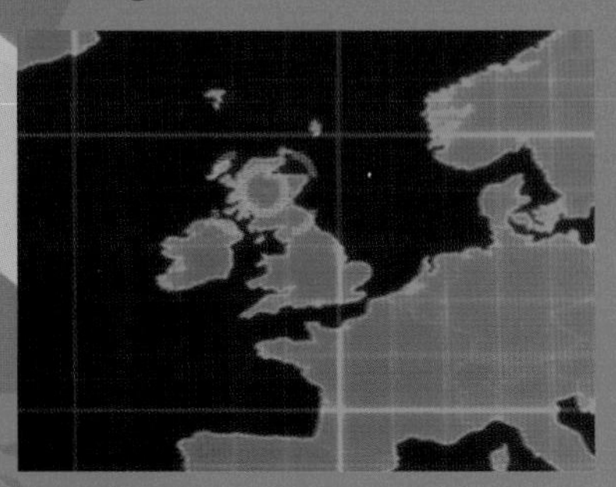

PREDATOR

The golden eagle is one of the largest, most impressive birds of prey. Its wings measure 2 metres or so from tip to tip when fully spread – that's longer than most people are tall. Despite its large size, the eagle is light – it has to be so that it can fly for long periods. Its bones have a honeycomb structure instead of being solid like ours, and its whole skeleton weighs only about 225 grams, less than a packet of butter. The eagle also has superb eyesight and super-sharp talons.

PREY

The hare, however, isn't an easy animal to catch. It runs at a blistering pace, reaching speeds of over 50 kilometres an hour. Most of the hare's muscle power is in its rear limbs and it leaps along in huge 2 metre bounds. The hare is also agile and is able to bob and weave and change direction with ease, sometimes succeeding in throwing the eagle off course.

THE ACTION

An eagle is soaring high above the ground as it searches for food. The huge surface area of its wings generates lots of lift so it hardly needs to flap them at all, which saves energy. It uses its tail to help with balance and steering.

A hare is hiding in the heather far below, relying on good camouflage to keep it hidden. It has become aware of the eagle but its first strategy is to stay very still and hope it isn't spotted.

But the eagle has noticed the hare and begins to line itself up for a killing swoop. At the last minute, though, the hare sneaks a short distance up the hill just as the eagle plunges – and misses its target.

As the eagle flies back up into the air the hare begins to run. Now the eagle can track its prey. Despite the hare's speed and agility there is no escaping this mighty bird. It chooses its moment, then rockets down towards the hare with its feet held at the ready.

It pounces on the hare, stabbing it with its killing talons, and this particular battle is over. The hare put up a good fight but this time it couldn't beat the eagle's strength and skill.

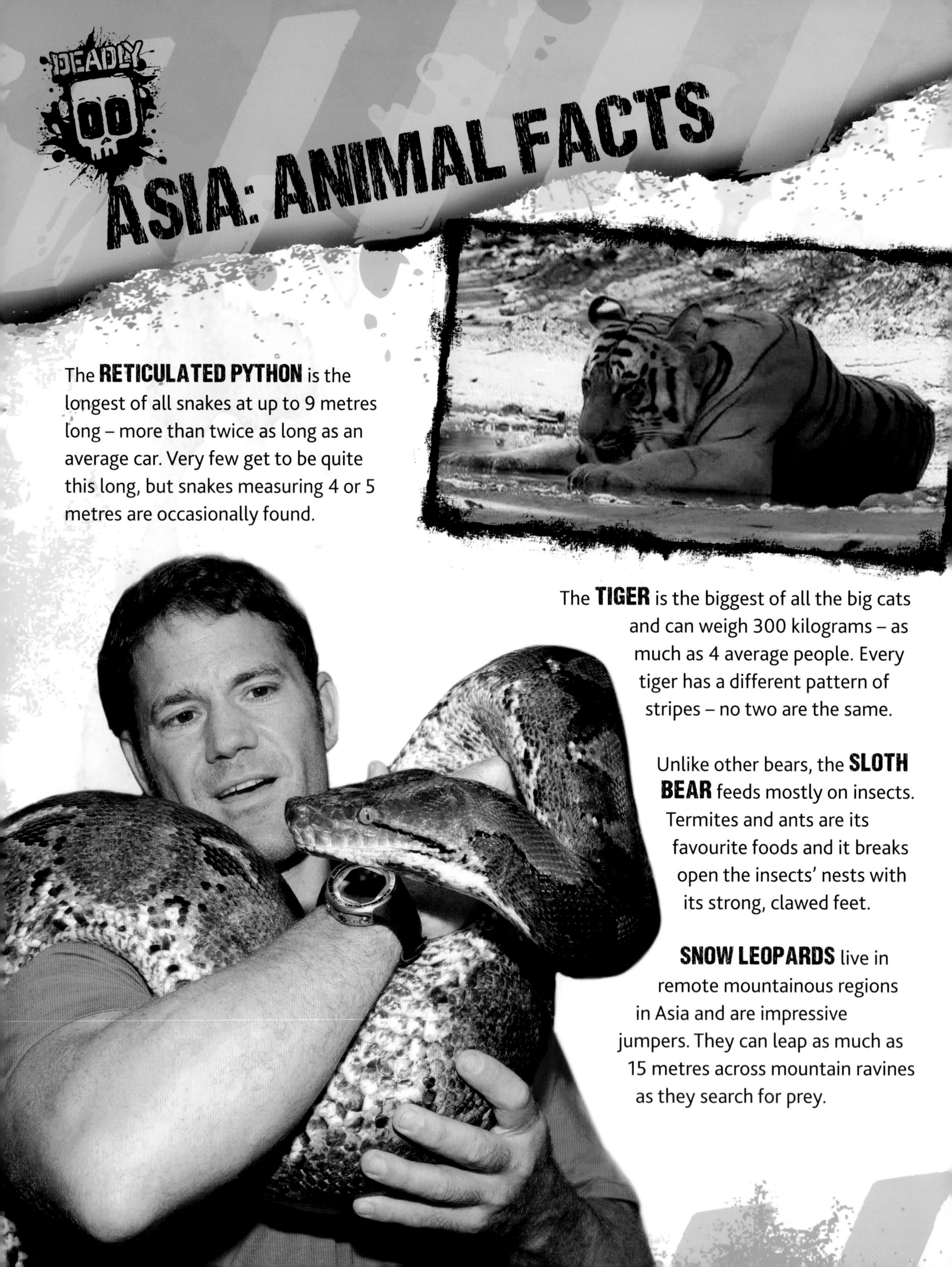

ASIA: ANIMAL FACTS

The **RETICULATED PYTHON** is the longest of all snakes at up to 9 metres long – more than twice as long as an average car. Very few get to be quite this long, but snakes measuring 4 or 5 metres are occasionally found.

The **TIGER** is the biggest of all the big cats and can weigh 300 kilograms – as much as 4 average people. Every tiger has a different pattern of stripes – no two are the same.

Unlike other bears, the **SLOTH BEAR** feeds mostly on insects. Termites and ants are its favourite foods and it breaks open the insects' nests with its strong, clawed feet.

SNOW LEOPARDS live in remote mountainous regions in Asia and are impressive jumpers. They can leap as much as 15 metres across mountain ravines as they search for prey.

One of the largest of all crocodiles, the **GHARIAL** can grow to 6 metres long. It has a longer and narrower snout than any other crocodile – ideally shaped for seizing slippery fish from the water.

The **TARSIER** is a tiny primate – a distant relative of monkeys and apes. Some species weigh only 100 grams, about as much as an apple. It hunts at night and has huge eyes. In fact, each eye is the same size as the tarsier's brain.

Mighty **KING COBRAS** are the longest of all venomous snakes. Some can measure an incredible 5.5 metres. A cobra's favourite prey is other snakes. It can deliver enough venom in a bite to kill an elephant.

The longest known insect in the world is a **STICK INSECT** that lives in Borneo. It is an amazing 56.7 centimetres long.

The **INDIAN RHINOCEROS** has a single horn on its head that can grow up to 57 centimetres long. Rhinos are among the biggest of all land animals and the Indian rhinoceros is the largest of the 3 species of rhino found in Asia. A full-grown male can weigh a hefty 2,200 kilograms.

STEVE WATCHING KOMODO DRAGONS AS THEY FEED.

ASIAN ANIMAL WORDSEARCH

DEADLY 60

These are just some of the incredible creatures that live in Asia. Can you find their names in this wordsearch?

K	R	E	E	A	I	R	I	R	N	A	K	R	N	F
O	T	O	I	O	N	N	I	U	I	H	I	E	I	E
M	A	S	T	E	F	O	A	E	D	S	N	G	L	H
O	R	Q	N	I	O	Y	D	E	N	T	G	I	O	S
D	S	Y	D	O	N	O	R	O	A	T	C	T	G	I
O	I	G	R	R	L	O	W	K	S	E	O	L	N	F
D	E	C	I	A	A	L	M	Y	I	S	B	A	A	N
R	R	O	R	A	E	E	C	R	M	I	R	G	P	O
A	G	I	S	O	N	E	B	D	E	E	A	N	C	I
G	H	S	P	E	O	T	A	H	R	T	O	E	T	L
O	A	A	T	P	R	A	P	E	T	I	A	B	H	O
N	R	O	K	C	E	G	Y	A	K	O	T	W	D	E
D	I	E	O	T	C	N	E	L	N	N	L	A	I	R
N	A	A	N	N	T	R	U	N	H	D	T	S	E	S
O	L	R	O	M	D	I	G	S	U	R	A	N	T	E

GHARIAL
PANGOLIN
TOKAY GECKO
GIANT PANDA

SLOTH BEAR
TARSIER
SNOW LEOPARD
LIONFISH

BENGAL TIGER
KING COBRA
WATER MONITOR
KOMODO DRAGON

DEADLY 60

PORTRAIT OF A PREDATOR: KOMODO DRAGON

The komodo dragon is a top predator on the Indonesian islands where it lives. The biggest lizard in the world, the komodo is up to 3.1 metres long and weighs as much as 166 kilograms.

This giant lizard is a huge powerful animal but it also has a venomous bite that helps it kill large prey, including deer, water buffalo and pigs. The venom prevents the victim's blood clotting and lowers its blood pressure. Even if the animal manages to escape the dragon's clutches it soon dies, and the dragon can catch up with it and feed at leisure.

Komodo dragons have big appetites and can eat up to 80 per cent of their body weight in one meal. They also devour carrion and can sniff out a meal from 10 kilometres away.

In the mating season, male komodos take part in battles over females. Supporting themselves on their strong tails, the males rear up and engage in fierce wrestling matches.

Venom gland in jaw.
Strong stocky legs.
Keen sense of smell.
Forked tongue.

DEADLY SPECIAL: TOP 10 KILLER TACTICS

Here is the Deadly team's list of the top 10 killer tactics used by animals to catch food. They involve surprise, stealth and even trickery.

HUMPBACK WHALE

Killer tactic:
superb teamwork

Humpbacks are the ultimate strategic predators, using a combination of teamwork and intelligence to catch their prey. In summer, humpbacks travel to the Pacific coast of North America to feast on huge shoals of herring. Several whales dive underwater and blow bubbles which form a ring and trap the fish. The whales then swoop up through the centre of the 'bubble net', engulfing the fish in their huge mouths.

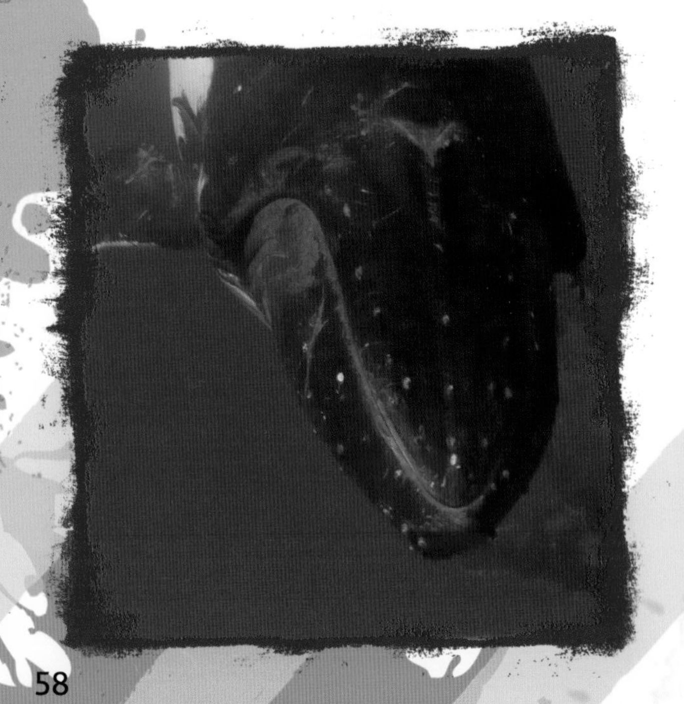

LEOPARD

Killer tactics:
stealth and strength

This big cat is one of the most skilful stalkers in the animal kingdom. It often hunts at night, creeping up soundlessly on animals such as deer or antelope. These creatures have acute hearing so the leopard has to move silently to get close to its prey. It makes every move with the utmost care and even controls its breathing. When it is as close as possible, the leopard pounces. If it succeeds in making the kill it then drags its prey up into a tree where it can feast in peace, safe from other hunters like lions who may want to steal the kill for themselves.

ALLIGATOR SNAPPING TURTLE

Killer tactic:
worm-like lure

The alligator snapping turtle lives in the swamps of the southern United States and is probably the biggest freshwater turtle in the world. It has stupendously powerful jaws which crunch up the toughest of prey. But that's not all; on its tongue is a fleshy growth that looks just like a tasty worm to a hungry fish. The turtle wiggles this lure, the fish comes closer to investigate – and the turtle's jaws slam shut around it.

GLADIATOR SPIDER

Killer tactic:
mobile web

This spider spins a web of very elastic silk to make a special kind of trap. Holding the web between its front legs, the spider hangs just above the ground from a convenient plant. When an unsuspecting insect walks by, the spider swiftly spreads its legs and net over it and wraps it up – ready for dinner.

STOAT

Killer tactic:
deadly dance moves

Stoats are fast runners and often chase their prey until it is exhausted and easily overcome. But sometimes the stoat tries a very different approach, darting and leaping around like a super-charged hip-hop dancer in front of a rabbit – a favourite prey. Incredibly the rabbit seems mesmerised by this performance and stands watching instead of making a quick escape. Mid-dance, the stoat chooses its moment to pounce and kill its victim, which may be more than 8 times its own weight, with a speedy bite.

CHIMPANZEE

Killer tactic: trap-setting skills

Chimps eat plants and fruit but they also hunt for meat. It's the males who hunt and they go after colobus monkeys. By working together and planning ahead, the troop can drive the colobus from its safe haven high in the trees straight into the jaws of other members of the gang.

7 GARTER SNAKE

Killer tactic: tongue trick

Adult garter snakes often feed on salamanders but younger individuals have developed their own feeding methods. The young snake flickers its tongue on the surface of the water, which to a hungry fish looks like a wriggling insect. When a fish comes to investigate it is swiftly snapped up by the cunning snake. Job done.

LEAF-TAILED GECKO

Killer tactic: invisibility

The gecko's perfect camouflage keeps it safe from predators while it watches out for its own prey. It is almost impossible to see as it clings to a tree trunk, where its irregular shape and mottled colouration helps it blend with its surroundings. The gecko can jump with lightning speed to catch prey or escape from danger.

9 AFRICAN WILD DOG

Killer tactic: pack hunting

These dogs hunt super-fast prey such as impala. They may start by moving as close as possible to their prey, aided by their multi-patterned coats that help camouflage them in vegetation. But the impala have excellent hearing and the slightest sound from the dogs sets the herd running. The dogs pursue at top speeds of up to 55 kilometres an hour and can run for great distances. Working together they eventually separate an animal from the rest of the herd and go in for the kill.

HARRIS HAWK

Killer tactic: teamwork

Most birds of prey hunt alone but these hawks, which live in parts of North and South America, can hunt in groups. This allows them to catch larger prey than they could manage alone. A group of 3 to 5 birds work together to flush out an animal such as a rabbit and then take turns to strike it. One bird may chase the prey on the ground while another swoops down from the air.

AUSTRALASIA ANIMAL FACTS

The **BOX JELLYFISH** kills more people in Australian waters than any other animal and may be the most venomous of all creatures. Its tentacles are up to 3 metres long and each is lined with as many as 5,000 stinging cells.

An **AUSTRALIAN TIGER BEETLE** can run faster than any other insect. It moves at about 2.5 metres a second – that's around 9 kilometres an hour.

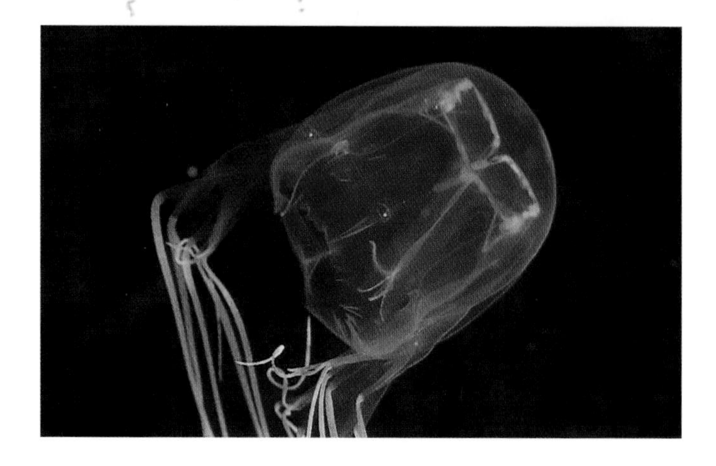

The **BLUE-RINGED OCTOPUS** is tiny but deadly. Its body is only 5 centimetres across and it weighs only 28 grams – not much more than a mouse – but it can kill a person with its venomous bite. Generally, though, it uses its venom to paralyse crabs and other prey.

The **INLAND TAIPAN** is considered to be the most venomous of all snakes. It preys on rats, mice and birds. Experts believe that the venom in just one bite from this deadly snake could kill 100 people.

The largest living carnivorous marsupial, the **TASMANIAN DEVIL** has such powerful jaws and teeth that it can crunch through bones. It does kill prey such as snakes, birds and fish but feeds mostly on carrion.

A full-grown Tasmanian devil is up to 80 centimetres long and can weigh as much as 12 kilograms.

The **PLATYPUS** is one of the very few mammals that lays eggs instead of giving birth to live young. It shelters in a burrow in the riverbank during the day but comes out at night to search for prey, including shellfish, insects and worms in the water. Its beak is extraordinarily sensitive and has special electro-receptors to pick up the tiniest muscle movements of its prey.

The male platypus has a sharp spur on each ankle that is linked to a venom gland. It uses its venomous spurs to defend itself against enemies and in battles with rival males. The venom can cause severe pain to a human and is said to be strong enough to kill a small dog.

The **SALTWATER CROCODILE** is the largest member of the crocodile family and the biggest of all reptiles. An average male saltie weighs up to 600 kilograms but giants of more than 1,000 kilograms have been recorded.

RED KANGAROOS are the largest of all marsupials. They are champion leapers and can jump more than 10 metres in a single bound.

Kangaroos are plant eaters, not predators. But they are big strong animals and can land a powerful kick with their back legs. Males sometimes have 'boxing matches' with rivals.

REDBACKS are highly venomous spiders. They are pretty small – the female's body is about 1 centimetre long and the male is only 4 millimetres – but the female's bite can be dangerous to humans.

QUOLLS are carnivorous marsupials. Although a quoll grows to only about 50 centimetres long with a tail of about the same length, it is a ferocious hunter with sharp pointed teeth for killing prey. It feeds on other marsupials, including possums, as well as on reptiles, birds and insects.

The **SAND GOANNA** is a lizard that lives in the Australian desert. A fast-moving predator, it will eat almost anything it can catch, including scorpions. Fortunately the lizard seems to be immune to the scorpion's venom.

The **KEA** is a most unusual parrot which lives only in New Zealand. It is thought to be one of the most intelligent of all birds and adapts quickly to changes in its environment. Keas eat seeds and insects but they also prey on young birds such as shearwaters. They dig the chicks out from their burrows and kill them with their sharply curved beak.

DEADLY 60

AUSTRALASIAN WORD SCRAMBLE

Can you unscramble the names of these animals? They all live in Australia or New Zealand.

gteri eteble
(Fast-running insect)

uried-gnlbe uotopcs
(Small but deadly sea creature)

tweatrsal ciocedlor
(Largest reptile)

ekdbarc idsper
(Small but deadly 8-legged creature)

aatminnas elivd
(Large carnivorous marsupial)

adinnl tpnaia
(Very venomous snake)

ulolq
(Small carnivorous marsupial)

uystppla
(Egg-laying mammal)

eka
(Intelligent bird)

edr gaokrnao
(Largest marsupial)

oxb slifejhly
(Water-living killer)

DEADLY SPECIAL: ANIMALS IN DANGER

Even the toughest, fiercest animals can come under threat when their habitat is disturbed or they are affected by hunting, pollution and other problems. Animals are said to be endangered when their numbers drop dangerously low – so low that they are at risk of becoming extinct and disappearing for ever from the wild. Some of the world's most magnificent creatures, like tigers and rhinos, are seriously endangered. Here are some others that we have been lucky enough to film on Deadly 60.

ETHIOPIAN WOLF

This wolf lives in the mountains of Ethiopia and is now the rarest member of the dog family, with a population of 500 at most in the wild. The wolves have been hunted in the past and more recently have suffered from diseases, such as rabies transmitted by domestic dogs. Now the main problem is habitat loss. The human population of Ethiopia has expanded rapidly and as people take over the land for farming there is less and less space for the wolves. They live in the high mountain ranges and are forced to compete for territory and prey.

Measures to protect the wolves are in place. Dogs are being vaccinated to control the spread of rabies, and protected areas have been established where the wolves can live. Conservation organisations are monitoring the situation closely to try to ensure that this wolf, one of the rarest of all mammals, survives.

SEA OTTER

Sea otters were hunted for their dense warm fur. So many were killed in the past that the species was on the edge of extinction. Now that hunting has been banned sea otter populations are on the increase.

There are other threats to their safety, however, including oil spills and other pollution, and they're still considered to be endangered.

WHALES

Whales have long been hunted for their meat, fat and oils. Although in 1986 commercial whaling was banned, some hunting has continued and 7 of the 13 species of great whale are now endangered or vulnerable to extinction.

Even the blue whale, the largest creature ever known to have lived on our planet, has been killed in its thousands. Scientists believe that blue whales are now among the rarest of the great whales. They are harmed by pollution and climate change and are also injured by ships and fishing equipment. Conservationists are working to reduce threats to the whales and numbers of some, such as humpbacks, are on the increase. Whale-watching trips are becoming very popular and some countries are realising that they can make more money from whale tourism than whale hunting.

GORILLAS

Gorillas are the world's largest primate. They feed only on plants but they are massively strong, powerful animals. They are not hunters but they will fight to the death to protect their family from danger.

Mountain gorillas live in a few small areas of Africa and their numbers are dangerously low. Teams of forest rangers and vets monitor the gorillas' every move and do their best to keep the remaining animals safe. Anti-poaching squads protect them from hunters and scientists study their behaviour.

STEVE IN A DIVING CAGE WATCHING A GREAT WHITE SHARK.

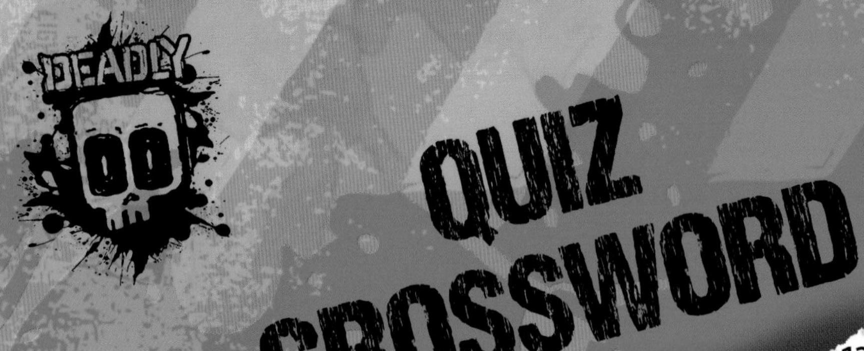

Work out the answers to this wildlife quiz and use them to fill in the crossword puzzle. You'll find the answers to the questions somewhere in this annual.

1 Across
Which is the fastest running animal in North America?
a Cheetah
b Pronghorn
c Bison

7 Across
What is the aye-aye's most important lethal weapon?
a Teeth
b Claws
c Finger

9 Across
What kind of creature is a tarsier?
a Insect
b Primate
c Seabird

10 Across and 6 Across
Which predator does the Deadly team think has the best killer tactics?
a Gladiator spider
b Harris hawk
c Humpback whale

11 Across and 6 Down
Which is the rarest member of the dog family?
a Grey wolf
b Ethiopian wolf
c Fennec fox

13 Across
Where does the spectacled bear live?
a Africa
b Australia
c South America

1 Down and 12 Across
Which predator does the Deadly team think has the best lethal weapons?
a Grizzly bear
b Praying mantis
c Bullet ant

2 Down
Which is the largest cat in South America?
a Jaguar
b Tiger
c Lion

3 Down and 9 Down
Which is the longest of all snakes?
a Reticulated python
b Green anaconda
c Boa constrictor

4 Down
Which is the largest of all land mammals?
a African elephant
b Rhinoceros
c Hippopotamus

5 Down
What group of animals does the wolverine belong to?
a Weasels
b Dogs
c Bats

8 Down
Which is the world's longest insect?
a Beetle
b Stick insect
c Grasshopper

Here you will find all the answers to the puzzles shown in this book!
Have fun now. . .

p27 CENTRAL & SOUTH AMERICAN ANIMAL WORDSEARCH

R	B	S	B	A	N	A	Q	T	O	C	E	L	O	T
I	E	U	L	V	E	D	Z	N	D	H	O	M	P	L
F	E	T	S	K	O	N	W	A	B	S	A	O	E	C
H	L	N	A	H	E	O	S	Y	Y	K	L	E	F	S
A	R	O	K	E	M	C	K	M	F	I	C	G	V	N
R	S	H	W	K	T	A	U	R	B	I	B	T	C	P
P	I	O	T	D	P	N	S	A	R	M	U	J	Y	R
Y	F	K	J	V	E	A	A	T	K	W	G	O	A	F
E	S	H	Z	N	I	N	C	T	E	C	U	U	O	B
A	M	F	V	O	H	E	A	E	N	R	G	E	H	W
G	D	G	M	N	L	E	X	M	B	A	A	F	C	Y
L	Z	P	H	E	S	R	C	I	J	Z	I	Y	O	Q
E	H	T	F	W	M	G	P	R	U	A	K	G	E	P
S	B	G	R	B	L	A	C	K	C	A	I	M	A	N
T	A	B	E	R	I	P	M	A	V	F	Y	S	B	R

p19 NORTH AMERICAN ANIMAL WORDSEARCH

N	E	M	C	Y	K	N	D	E	I	A	Q	R	A	P
O	N	R	T	O	A	N	T	T	L	R	F	A	E	S
I	I	F	E	E	T	S	U	L	E	L	S	E	L	R
L	R	M	E	T	L	T	I	K	O	A	T	B	G	E
N	E	U	H	I	T	G	O	W	S	T	F	K	A	T
I	V	B	A	C	A	O	Y	N	D	E	Y	C	E	S
A	L	F	M	T	O	E	A	O	M	D	O	A	D	N
T	O	R	O	H	R	E	T	E	E	O	P	L	L	O
N	W	R	H	G	I	C	A	T	S	R	U	B	A	M
U	E	K	A	N	S	E	L	T	T	A	R	T	B	A
O	P	O	L	A	R	B	E	A	R	C	N	E	H	L
M	X	O	F	C	I	T	C	R	A	C	I	E	U	I
T	L	H	H	X	N	I	C	R	L	O	F	Y	O	G
E	O	F	R	A	S	T	N	A	W	O	A	E	A	O
M	N	A	E	E	N	A	I	T	U	N	S	T	N	S

p37 AFRICAN ANIMALS CRISS CROSS

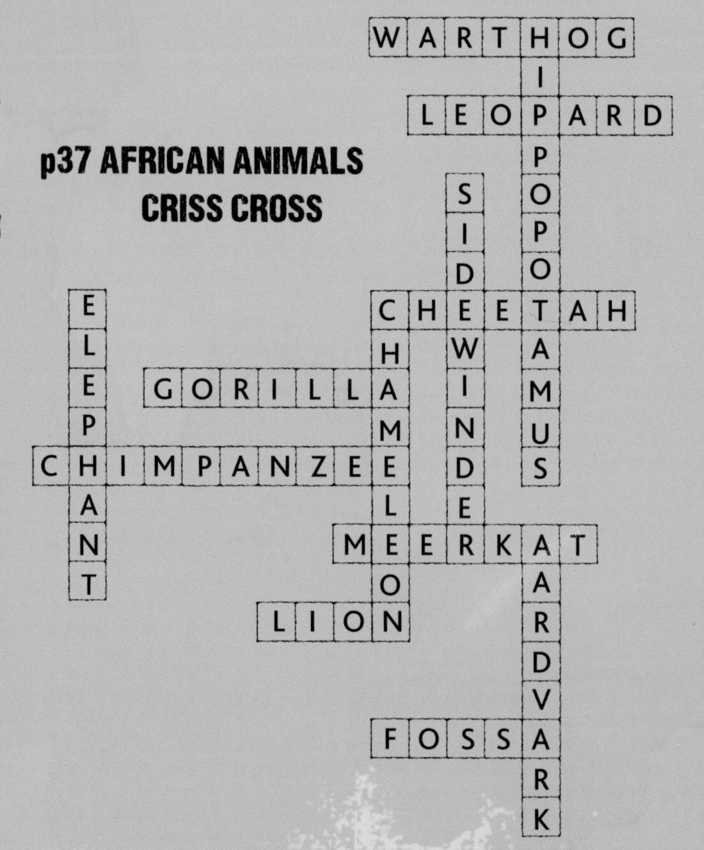

p45 EUROPEAN ANIMAL WORDSEARCH

S	R	L	C	R	T	N	N	D	L	C	T	F	M	N
I	X	A	O	E	H	F	R	S	R	E	D	E	W	I
R	O	H	N	R	L	A	R	A	C	H	A	T	E	A
U	O	N	H	E	G	H	B	O	I	A	E	E	A	R
I	A	R	M	O	A	S	N	K	X	N	Y	L	E	W
G	I	O	N	S	P	G	O	Y	W	S	T	M	T	O
E	L	F	E	I	E	A	H	T	C	A	T	R	H	D
O	L	K	D	R	H	O	R	N	E	T	H	C	I	R
Y	I	E	E	A	I	A	H	D	N	M	N	S	N	R
P	R	E	L	E	R	T	S	E	K	R	T	E	O	S
O	L	U	E	S	E	L	P	A	E	C	E	R	N	G
E	L	G	A	E	Y	N	W	A	T	M	E	D	T	M
E	E	C	I	E	R	H	H	E	A	T	N	P	D	S
T	O	R	S	T	O	I	O	N	T	M	S	C	R	A
M	I	D	W	T	D	T	A	O	O	D	I	H	N	T

p55 ASIAN ANIMAL WORDSEARCH

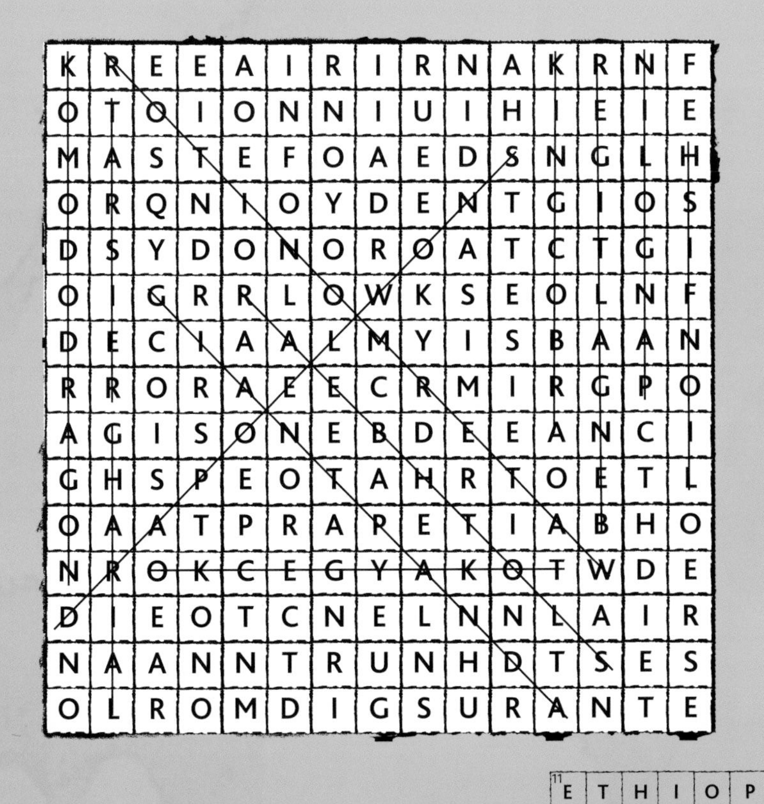

K	R	E	E	A	I	R	I	R	N	A	K	R	N	F
O	T	O	I	O	N	N	I	U	I	H	I	E	I	E
M	A	S	T	E	F	O	A	E	D	S	N	G	L	H
O	R	Q	N	I	O	Y	D	E	N	T	G	I	O	S
D	S	Y	D	O	N	O	R	O	A	T	C	T	G	I
O	I	G	R	R	L	O	W	K	S	E	O	L	N	F
D	E	C	I	A	A	L	M	Y	I	S	B	A	A	N
R	R	O	R	A	E	E	C	R	M	I	R	G	P	O
A	G	I	S	O	N	E	B	D	E	E	A	N	C	I
G	H	S	P	E	O	T	A	H	R	T	O	E	T	L
O	A	A	T	P	R	A	P	E	T	I	A	B	H	O
N	R	O	K	C	E	G	Y	A	K	O	T	W	D	E
D	I	E	O	T	C	N	E	L	N	N	L	A	I	R
N	A	A	N	N	T	R	U	N	H	D	T	S	E	S
O	L	R	O	M	D	I	G	S	U	R	A	N	T	E

p65 AUSTRALASIAN WORD SCRAMBLE

Tiger beetle (fast-running insect)

Blue-ringed octopus (small but deadly sea creature)

Saltwater crocodile (largest reptile)

Redback spider (small but deadly 8-legged creature)

Tasmanian devil (large carnivorous marsupial)

Inland taipan (very venomous snake)

Quoll (small carnivorous marsupial)

Platypus (egg-laying mammal)

Kea (intelligent bird)

Red kangaroo (largest marsupial)

Box jellyfish (water-living killer)

p70 QUIZ CROSSWORD

STEVE WITH AN
EGYPTIAN VULTURE.

DEADLY